Praise for The American Way

I appreciate this book because too many people get sucked in to MLM's. And these companies would have you believe you can get rich! Quit your 9-5! And live a lifestyle most only ever dream of living!

The truth is they are just scamming you and the only people getting rich are those at the top while the ones at the bottom go into debt! Then they are told they just aren't working hard enough! It's a sad cycle that seems to keep regenerating over and over again.

The author gives us his brief (thank god it was brief) experience in Amway and was smart enough to not only get out quickly but is now trying to educate others to not be sucked into Amway or any other MLM.

Done so in a very respectful way I might add.

~ Emily D.

More books by Ian Schrauth

The Opportunity
The Short-lived Social media biz of Darleen Hoffman

A heart of fate and love
Till I Find You
Call me maybe: Vol. 1

SLMPD

Within the air
Trace My Steps
The American Way
Beyond the Veil

The American Way

The Good, the Bad, and the Lies I've learned from Being an Amway IBO

IAN
BESTSELLING AUTHOR
SCHRAUTH

Copyright © 2019 by Starboat, LLC
Cover and internal design © 2023 by HeartStone Virtual Solutions, LLC
Cover designed by Starboat, LLC

All rights reserved. No part of this book may be reproduced in any form or by any electronic or mechanical means, including information storage and retrieval systems, without written permission from the author.

The characters and events portrayed in this book are fictitious or are used fictitiously. Any similarity to a real persons, living or dead, is purely confidential. And not intended by the author.

All brand names and product names used in this book are trademarks, registered trademarks, or trade names of their represented holders. Starboat, LLC and the author are not associated with any product or vendor in the book.

Printed by Amazon Kindle Direct Publishing

LSC 10 9 8 7 6

Note from the author

This books is based on my own experiences with Amway, and research I have done from independent/researched sources.

All of the information in this book was verified beforehand.

Just because you don't like to hear this information, doesn't mean it's false.

Preface

Back in 2018, I wanted to create my own mobile application

So, I decided to sit down and make the app and started to do some pre-release promotion on a Facebook group, dedicated to people in my township

I was getting comments on the post, asking when it would be released, and how they can help, but I also got a message from one of my friends from grade school, asking if I was an entrepreneur.

Of course, I said yes and he said he was too. Soon afterwards, he invited me to some stranger's house, so that I can listen to his "business plan". I went to their house, and fast forward to a couple of months, he got me. I fell into his multi-level-marketing trap. I paid the

$62 out of my own savings account and started selling some products.

When I first started, I was clueless. I was totally sucked into the "business". I was giving out business cards with my information on it, I was buying products, and I was bugging my friends on social media about this "amazing business opportunity". I even told my upline that I wanted to make this a full-time carrier.

Because it's true…mostly

I want to own my own business and be my own boss, but doing this came out to be FAR from that.

Two months later, I sent in my resignation letter to Amway, stating that I am no longer going to be selling their products as an "independent business owner", and I have never felt so happier in my life after I took this decision.

Luckily, I didn't spend too much money. I got my refund for my $62, and I was out of reach of the Multi-level-marketing cult-like tactics.

I hope you enjoy this small book, about what I learned throughout my small journey through being in a multi-level-marketing company as a so-called "independent business owner". It will tell you all you need to know about the business, and then you can make a decision if you want to join, or if it's a pass.

Thank you,

Ian Schrauth
Bestselling Author

The History

Introduction

Before we can go into he good, the bad, and the lies about the company, we first have to dig deep into the history of Amway.

What is Multi-Level Marketing (MLM)?

Multi-level Marketing, or MLM for short, is a marketing strategy where companies recruit individuals to sell products or services to their friends, family, and acquaintances while also recruiting new members to join the company. The primary goal of MLM is to create a network of distributors, which often consists of people who have little or no experience in sales.

While MLMs have been promoted as a path to financial freedom, many individuals who join these companies often find themselves in debt or unable to make a profit.

One of the primary appeals of MLMs is the promise of financial freedom. Distributors are often promised large incomes, luxurious lifestyles, and the ability to work from home. MLMs also appeal to individuals who are looking for a low-risk business opportunity, as the start-up costs are often minimal. However, these promises are often unrealistic, and many individuals who join MLMs end up losing money instead of making it.

According to the Federal Trade Commission (FTC), over 99% of individuals who join MLMs do not make a profit. This is because MLMs rely on a constant influx of new recruits to make money. Distributors are often required to purchase large quantities of products in order to meet sales quotas, which can result in debt if they are unable to sell the products. Additionally, distributors are often encouraged to recruit new members to join the company, which can lead to a saturated market and fierce competition among distributors.

MLMs are often criticized for their predatory nature. Distributors are encouraged to target their friends, family, and acquaintances, often putting a strain on these relationships. Distributors are also often required to attend training sessions and purchase motivational materials, which can be expensive and do not necessarily provide any real value. In some cases, MLMs have been compared to pyramid schemes, which are illegal.

According to the National Association of Consumer Advocates (NACA), MLMs are mathematically impossible for everyone to make money. This is because MLMs rely on a never-ending chain of recruitment, which is unsustainable. While it is true that some individuals may make money in the short term, the vast majority of distributors will not be able to make a profit in the long run. The only individuals who stand to benefit from MLMs are those at the top of the pyramid, who earn money from the recruitment and sales efforts of those below them.

In addition to being unsustainable, MLMs often use deceptive marketing tactics to lure in new recruits. Distributors are often promised large incomes, luxurious lifestyles, and the ability to work from home, without any mention of the risks involved. MLMs often use vague and misleading language to describe their products and compensation plans, making it difficult for individuals to make informed decisions.

Despite these criticisms, MLMs continue to be popular in many countries around the world. In the United States, MLMs are regulated by the FTC, which has brought numerous enforcement actions against companies that engage in deceptive practices. However, MLMs continue to operate and recruit new members, often targeting vulnerable individuals who are looking for a way to make extra money.

Who is Amway?

Amway, also known as the American Way Association, is an MLM that sells health, beauty, and home care products.

The company was founded in 1959 by Jay Van Andel and Rich DeVos and is headquartered in Ada, Michigan. In this essay, we will explore the history of Amway, including its political history and donations.

Jay Van Andel and Rich DeVos, childhood friends from Grand Rapids, Michigan, started Amway in 1959. The company's first product was a liquid organic cleaner called Frisk, which they sold door-to-door. Amway's business model was based on direct selling and multi-level marketing, where independent distributors sold products to their friends and family, while also recruiting new distributors to join the company. Amway's initial success came from its unique business model, which allowed individuals to start their own business with minimal start-up costs.

Amway grew quickly, and by the mid-1960s, the company had expanded internationally, with operations in Canada, Australia, and the United Kingdom. In the 1970s, Amway launched a new line of products, including Nutrilite, a line of health supplements, and Artistry, a line of beauty products. The company continued to expand throughout the 1980s and 1990s, and today, Amway operates in more than 100 countries worldwide.

Despite its success, Amway has faced numerous controversies throughout its history. In the 1970s, Amway was accused of operating as a pyramid scheme, with distributors earning more money from recruiting new members than from selling products. Amway denied the allegations and took legal action against the Federal Trade Commission (FTC), which had launched an investigation into the company's business practices. The case was eventually settled in 1979, with Amway agreeing to make changes to its compensation plan to address concerns about pyramid schemes.

In the 1990s, Amway faced another controversy, this time related to its business practices in China. Amway had been operating in China since 1995, but in 1998, the Chinese government launched an investigation into the company's sales practices. The investigation revealed that Amway had been operating as an illegal pyramid scheme, and the company was fined $7.8 million. Amway denied the allegations and continued to operate in China, but the controversy damaged the company's reputation and sales in the country.

Amway's political history is also worth exploring. The company has a long history of political donations, with many of its executives and employees contributing to political campaigns and causes. According to the Center for Responsive Politics, Amway has donated more than $13 million to political candidates and causes since 1990. The majority of these donations have gone to Republican candidates and causes, with only a small percentage going to Democratic candidates.

One of Amway's most prominent political donations was to the Christian conservative organization Focus on the Family. According to Forbes, the DeVos family, who co-founded Amway, donated more than $5 million to Focus on the Family between 1997 and 2001. Focus on the Family is a controversial organization that has been criticized for its opposition to LGBT rights and its promotion of "conversion therapy," a practice that attempts to change a person's sexual orientation.

Amway has also been criticized for its involvement in political lobbying. According to the Center for Responsive Politics, Amway spent more than $2.5 million on lobbying efforts in 2020, with the majority of its efforts focused on issues related to international trade and taxes. Amway has lobbied on behalf of the Direct Selling Association, a trade group that represents multi-level marketing companies.

In 2010, Amway was named one of the top polluters in Michigan by the Michigan Department of Environmental Quality. The company was found to have violated environmental regulations at its manufacturing plant in Ada, Michigan, where it produces many of its cleaning and personal care products. Amway has since taken steps to improve its environmental record, including reducing its greenhouse gas emissions and implementing a sustainability program.

Despite its controversies, Amway has maintained a loyal following of distributors and customers. The company's business model, which allows individuals to start their own business with minimal start-up costs, has been attractive to many people looking for a flexible and entrepreneurial opportunity. Amway's product line, which includes health supplements, beauty products, and home care items, has also been popular with consumers.

Despite its loyal following, however, Amway's business model has been criticized by some as predatory and mathematically impossible for everyone to make money. According to a study by the Consumer Awareness Institute, more than 99% of Amway distributors lose money, with only a small percentage earning enough to make a living. The study found that the vast majority of Amway distributors earn less than $100 per month, while the top earners make millions of dollars per year.

Critics of MLM companies argue that these companies are inherently exploitative, as they rely on distributors to recruit new members to the company in order to earn commissions. This creates a pyramid-like structure, where the majority of the earnings go to the top-level distributors, while those at the bottom struggle to make any money at all. This structure also puts pressure on distributors to recruit as many people as possible, even if it means selling products to people who do not want or need them.

Amway and the politics

Amway's involvement in politics can be traced back to the company's early years. Richard Devos and Jay Van Andel were both active in the Republican Party, and they used their wealth and influence to support conservative causes. In 1975, Devos ran for governor of Michigan as a Republican but was defeated by the incumbent Democrat. Despite the loss, Devos continued to be involved in politics and used his wealth to support conservative candidates and causes.

In the 1980s, Amway began to expand its operations internationally, and the company's political influence grew as well. Amway executives and IBOs became involved in political campaigns in countries such as Canada and Australia, supporting conservative candidates who were seen as friendly to Amway's business interests. In 1983, Amway Australia was embroiled in a political scandal when it was revealed that the company had made illegal contributions to the Liberal Party of Australia. The scandal resulted in a Royal Commission investigation, which found that Amway had made over $1 million in illegal political contributions.

Amway's involvement in politics continued to grow in the 1990s, particularly in the United States. In 1992, Amway co-founder Jay Van Andel became a member of the President's Export Council under President George H.W. Bush. The Council was a group of business leaders who advised the President on issues related to international trade. Van Andel's appointment to the Council was seen as a sign of Amway's growing political influence.

Amway's involvement in politics has not been without controversy. Critics have accused the company of using its wealth and influence to advance conservative causes and to undermine labor unions and environmental regulations. In

1995, Amway was the subject of a congressional investigation into its political activities. The investigation focused on allegations that Amway had used its IBOs to promote conservative causes and to fund political campaigns. The investigation resulted in no charges being filed against Amway, but it did shed light on the company's political activities and raised questions about the role of direct-selling companies in politics.

In 2006, Amway was once again embroiled in a political scandal, this time in India. The company had been accused of bribing Indian officials in order to advance its business interests in the country. The scandal led to protests against Amway in India, and the company was eventually forced to suspend its operations in the country.

In the United States, Amway has been criticized for its support of conservative causes and for its involvement in the anti-union movement. The company has been a strong supporter of the Republican Party, and it has donated millions of dollars to conservative candidates and causes over the years. In 2012, Amway was the largest donor to the Republican National Convention, donating $2 million to the event.

Amway has also been criticized for its opposition to labor unions. The company has been involved in a number of labor disputes over the years, with critics accusing the company of using its wealth and influence to undermine union organizing efforts. In 2007, Amway was sued by the International Brotherhood of Teamsters, which accused the company of using illegal tactics to prevent workers from organizing. The lawsuit was settled in 2010, with Amway agreeing to pay $56 million in damages to the workers.

In addition to its opposition to labor unions, Amway has also been criticized for its stance on environmental regulations. The company has been a strong opponent of regulations that it sees as overly burdensome, particularly those related to the use of chemicals in its products. In 2011,

Amway was one of several companies that successfully lobbied the Michigan state government to weaken regulations on the use of phosphorus in household cleaning products.

Amway's involvement in politics has had a significant impact on the political landscape, particularly in the United States. The company's financial support for conservative candidates and causes has helped to advance the conservative agenda on a number of issues, including taxes, regulation, and labor rights. Amway's opposition to labor unions has also contributed to the decline of organized labor in the United States, which has had a ripple effect on a number of industries.

However, Amway's involvement in politics has also led to controversy and criticism, particularly from those who see the company's activities as an attempt to undermine democracy and the rule of law. Critics argue that Amway's use of its wealth and influence to advance conservative causes gives it an unfair advantage in the political process and undermines the ability of ordinary citizens to have their voices heard.

The Good

Introduction

Amway is one of those Multi-Level-Marketing (MLM) companies that offer a variety of products. Before I signed up for Amway, I took a look at my friend's Amway catalog. It was more than what my grandmother bought a long time ago. Back then, there were a lot of cleaning products in their catalog, and that was it. But now, they have a lot more products in their catalog. As an Independent Business Owner (IBO), you are required to sell these products, to make money, and to recruit three people into the business to make money.

Nutrition

According to the Amway website, the company offers products from a variety of brands including Nutriline, Double X, BodyKey, and XS. Nutriline, one of the main brands, specializes in vitamins and supplements, wellness bars, and more. The company claims that its products are made with high-quality ingredients and are scientifically formulated to meet the needs of its customers.

The XS line of products offered by Amway includes CocoWater, a drink mix for hydration, muscle multiplier, and energy drinks in various flavors such as root beer, blood orange, strawberry, cherry cola blast, and many others. The company markets its energy drinks as a healthier alternative to traditional energy drinks on the market. The XS energy drinks are marketed as containing less sugar and calories while still providing the energy boost that consumers need.

The Double X line of products is a subsidiary of Nutriline and offers dietary supplements. According to the company, the Double X supplements are made with a blend of 12 essential vitamins and 10 essential minerals that are designed to support overall health and wellness. The supplements are marketed as being easy to digest and provide a balanced dose of essential nutrients.

BodyKey is another subsidiary of Nutriline, which offers meal replacement shakes and bars, and various snacks. The company claims that its BodyKey products are designed to help customers achieve their weight management goals. The meal replacement shakes and bars are marketed as a convenient and healthy alternative to traditional meals.

However, despite the wide range of products offered by Amway, the company has been criticized for the quality of its products. According to a Forbes article, some of the products sold by Amway have been found to be of questionable quality, and some customers have reported experiencing negative side effects from using the products.

Beauty

Amway's beauty line is a collection of different beauty products that cater to beauty needs of both men and women.

Artistry offers a variety of skincare products for women, including cleansers, toners, moisturizers, serums, masques/exfoliators, and "intense" care products. These products are formulated with powerful and nourishing ingredients such as botanicals, vitamins, and antioxidants. The cleansers and toners work to remove dirt and impurities from the skin, while the moisturizers and serums work to hydrate, nourish, and protect the skin. The masques/exfoliators help to remove dead skin cells and impurities, revealing smoother and brighter-looking skin. The "intense" care products are specifically formulated to target specific skin concerns such as dark spots, fine lines, and wrinkles.

Artistry's makeup line is also extensive, offering a range of products for the face, cheeks, eyes, and lips. The face products include foundation, powder, and concealer, while the cheek products include blush and bronzer. The eye products include eyeshadow, eyeliner, mascara, and brow products, and the lip products include lipsticks, lip glosses, and lip liners. Additionally, Artistry offers makeup remover kits and accessories such as brushes, sponges, and applicators.

Artistry's Studio line is \designed for those who want to achieve a bold and dramatic look, such as pop stars. The Studio line includes vibrant eyeshadows, bold lip colors, and dramatic eyeliner.

For men, Artistry offers a variety of facial care products such as facial moisturizer, post-shave cream, shave cream, face wash, and serum concentrate. These products are formulated with powerful ingredients such as aloe vera, ginger root extract, and vitamin E, which work together to hydrate, soothe, and protect the skin.

Ian Schrauth

The American Way

Bath and Body products

Amway not only provides beauty and nutrition products, but they also cater to personal hygiene products. They have a range of products from three main brands - G&H, Glister, and Satinique.

The G&H brand is formulated to provide nourishment, hydration, and protection to the skin. They offer a range of sub-brands that cater to different skin types and concerns. The Nourish+ sub-brand hydrates the skin with body lotion, body wash, cream, and complexion bar (soap). The Refresh+ sub-brand revitalizes and soothes the skin with gel body wash and body milk. The Protect+ sub-brand protects the skin from environmental stressors with bar soap, concentrated hand soap, and deodorant.

The Glister brand focuses on oral care products, offering a variety of toothpaste, refresher spray, oral rinse, and toothbrushes.

These products are designed to promote oral health, leaving the mouth feeling fresh and clean.

The Satinique brand caters to hair care products. The products are formulated with a blend of botanicals, vitamins, and antioxidants, which work together to nourish, strengthen, and protect the hair. The Satinique collection includes a range of shampoos, conditioners, and styling products that cater to different hair types and concerns.

In addition to the main brands, Amway also offers a range of personal care products that cater to different needs. They offer a range of body washes, soaps, deodorants, and shaving creams for both men and women. These products are formulated with high-quality ingredients that nourish, hydrate, and protect the skin.

Home goods

Amway also offer a specialized brand named Amway Home, which caters to a wide range of home goods. The Amway Home brand provides customers with cleaning products that are specifically designed to meet their needs.

The Amway Home brand offers a range of products, including liquid and powder laundry detergent, fabric bleach, prewash spray, and fabric softener. The products are formulated with high-quality ingredients that are gentle on clothes and provide effective cleaning results. The brand is committed to ensuring that the products are environmentally friendly and do not contain any harmful chemicals that could be harmful to the environment or individuals.

Previously, Amway used to offer a Legacy At Home brand, which was designed to cater to customers' home cleaning needs. However, it seems that the brand has been discontinued.

The Bad

Introduction

Congratulations! You made the decision to become a "real business owner" and join Amway! But hold on there! Not only did you use the last of your paycheck to become a commission-only salesperson, there are some things you need to know before you start raking in that invisible cash…

Your startup

First and foremost, Amway's startup tactic relies heavily on recruiting friends and family members to join the business. While this may seem like a good way to start, it can quickly lead to problems. According to a report by the Federal Trade Commission, "the majority of people who join multi-level marketing companies (like Amway) lose money." This is because these types of businesses rely on a constant flow of new recruits to make money. As a result, many people who join end up losing money instead of making it.

Furthermore, Amway's startup tactic does not provide its members with the necessary tools and resources to run a successful business. According to an article by Forbes, "most Amway distributors are not taught how to sell the products or how to run a successful business." This lack of training can make it difficult for members to succeed and can lead to frustration and disappointment.

Another issue with Amway's startup tactic is that it requires members to pay a fee to join the business. While this fee may seem small, it can quickly add up. According to an article by The Balance Small Business, "Amway distributors are required to purchase a starter kit that costs between $62 and $188." This is a significant amount of money, especially for those who may be struggling financially.

Moreover, Amway's startup tactic relies heavily on hosting parties and events to sell products. While this may seem like a good way to generate sales, it can quickly become overwhelming. According to an article by The Atlantic, "Amway distributors are encouraged to host parties and invite friends and family members to attend." This can put a lot of pressure on members to constantly host events and can lead to burnout.

In addition, Amway's startup tactic requires members to study the products and get to know them. While this may seem like a good idea, it can be time-consuming and overwhelming. According to an article by The Balance Small Business, "Amway distributors are required to study the products and become experts in their field." This can be difficult for those who may not have a lot of experience in sales or marketing.

Grand opening Party

Amway, like many other MLM companies, relies heavily on the recruitment of new members to drive sales and generate profit. One way they do this is by hosting grand opening parties for new distributors.

These events are often portrayed as a fun and exciting way to kick off a new business venture, but in reality, they are just another tactic used by Amway to lure in unsuspecting individuals.

At these grand opening parties, the new member is expected to invite friends and family to attend. The purpose of these events is to showcase the Amway products and encourage attendees to make purchases. The new member is responsible for promoting the products and trying to convince their guests to become customers or even join the business themselves.

These grand opening parties are typically filled with scripted speeches, testimonials from successful Amway members, and high-pressure sales tactics. Attendees are often bombarded with pitches for the latest products, and the pressure to buy can be overwhelming. The new member is expected to be the host and lead the charge, often at their own expense.

I will say that in my grand opening party, my upline's upline did the most of the leg work for it. I did not have to spend a single penny on it.

The reality of these grand-opening parties is that they are a thinly veiled attempt to recruit new members and increase sales. Amway and other MLM companies often prey on vulnerable individuals who are looking for a way to make extra money or achieve financial freedom. These grand opening parties are designed to make people feel like they are

> It's also worth noting that not all Amway teams do a "Grand Opening" Party. Te team I was apart of was called "ILD Global", and they are a "break-off branch" off the "World Wide Dream Builders" (Abbreviated as "WWDB"). Because of their affiliation with WWDB, they mimic a lot

part of a community and part of something bigger, but in reality, they are just another tactic used to manipulate and exploit people

In addition to the high-pressure sales tactics, grand opening parties are often filled with misleading claims and promises. Amway distributors are often taught to exaggerate the earning potential of the business, promising large sums of money in a short amount of time. However, the reality is that very few people actually make a significant amount of money with Amway or any other MLM company.

<u>Bugging your friends/family</u>

What would happen if you were approached by your friend you haven't seen in High School for a long time, and told about an "amazing business opportunity" and you are told that you can get rich quick? How would you feel about this? Would you feel annoyed? Angry? Would you try to say no, only to have them block you? When you are recruited, you're required to make a list of your closest friends and family, and call them up to tell them about your business. You're required to promote the crap out of your "business" to try and either get sales or recruit people.

Cold messaging people

During my time in Amway, I was required to make a list of close friends, family, and acquaintances to share the "amazing opportunity" with. The idea was to reach out to as many people as possible and get them to sign up under me as my downline. However, when we ran out of people on our list, we were required to get creative. Amway encouraged us to create a LinkedIn profile, an Amazon Fan page, and even run Facebook ads for our "business" and invite people to the opportunity through social media.

Unfortunately, this was not the end of it. Many posts on Reddit's r/AntiMLM subreddit are filled with stories of Amway independent sales reps cold messaging people on social media, and even calling up friends-of-friends asking them to join in. It's no surprise that this type of behavior is not only annoying but can be extremely off-putting and pushy.

To top it all off, I was even approached by someone in a Barnes and Noble bookstore while browsing books in the business section. I'm not sure if they were associated with Amway, but the encounter left a bad taste in my mouth. It's not only frustrating to constantly be bombarded with people trying to sell you something, but it's also important to remember that not everyone is interested in joining an MLM company.

The pressure to constantly recruit new members is intense. We were told that the more people we signed up, the more money we could make. However, this mentality led to a lot of uncomfortable situations. I remember feeling guilty for not recruiting my friends and family members, but at the same time, I knew deep down that it wasn't a good idea to mix business with pleasure.

One of the most troubling aspects of being a part of Amway was the fact that I was required to buy products myself to sell. In order to make money, I had to purchase a certain amount of products each month, which put a strain on my finances. I remember feeling like I was constantly in debt because I was always buying products to sell, but not making enough money to cover my expenses.

In addition to the financial strain, there was also a lot of pressure to attend events and meetings. I was told that attending these events was crucial to my success, and that I would be missing out on important information if I didn't go. However, many of these events were expensive and time-consuming. It was frustrating to feel like I had to sacrifice my time and money in order to be successful in the business.

Making money

I thought to myself that I would become rich, and make it a full-time career. All of those are not the case. I ended up leaving in January of 2019. The idea of being rich was so far off into fantasy, it wasn't even funny. Every time, I would buy an $8 bottle of 9.4 fl. oz. shampoo from my own site, I would make $0.01 from it. My friend who recruited me, my upline, and their upline made the most money off me. Heck, it even made them bonuses. I know this because I was attending a "business" meeting at one point, and the couple at the Emerald rank were bragging about how they get so many bonuses because of this opportunity, and how they haven't been at a 9-5 job in however long. Not only did I realize that this was disgusting, but it was also unethical for me and their downline to be buying products, having people under them buy products, and having them reap the benefits.

Many people use Amway to pay some (or all) their bills. The only reason why they make so much money is because they started off early in the game, and they recruited people below them that sell/buy products and recruit others.

To make things worse about the pay, Amway is like almost every other MLM, where they pay weekly. I don't have a problem with jobs that pay weekly. MY 9-5 JOB pays me weekly. But the reason it's a problem within a Multi-Level Marketing company is because of how much they earn within that week. They spend a LOT of money, but a lot (if not all of it) goes right back to Amway in product purchases, paid advertisements, and other 1-099 contractor expenses. Because of this, getting paid weekly gives the illusion that they're paid more often. In reality, their paychecks are VERY low. One of my weekly paychecks was ONE PENNY!

The reproductions of leaving Amway

It's important to acknowledge that leaving Amway can come with its own set of challenges, particularly in regards to the reactions of former upline members. Many people who have left Amway have reported being harassed or talked about by their former upline, often because they feel threatened by the individual's departure from the company. This behavior is unacceptable and can be damaging to one's mental health and relationships.

It's important to remember that leaving Amway doesn't mean severing all ties with former upline members. Some people are fortunate enough to maintain friendly relationships with their former upline, as in the case of the author of this passage. However, this is not always the case, and it's important to set boundaries and prioritize one's own well-being in such situations.

It's also worth noting that the pressure to maintain these friendships can make it harder for people to leave the company. Many former members report feeling guilty or like they're letting their friends down by leaving Amway. This emotional manipulation is a tactic often used by MLMs to keep members in the company, even when it's no longer in their best interest.

The recruitment

Amway markets itself as a way for people to start their own business and become financially independent. The company sells a wide range of products, from home care and personal care to health and wellness. However, the primary way that people make money through Amway is by recruiting others to join the company and build a downline. The more people they recruit, the more money they make. This is the basis of the MLM business model.

One of the main reasons why Amway recruits people is because they know that there are many people out there who are in need of money. Whether it's due to a job loss, unexpected expenses, or a desire to make more money, there are countless people who are struggling financially. Amway targets these people by promising them a way to make money quickly and easily. They promise that if they just recruit a few people and build a downline, they will be able to make a significant amount of money without having to work too hard.

However, the reality is that very few people actually make money through Amway. According to a report by the Federal Trade Commission, less than 1% of people who join MLM companies like Amway actually make a profit. The vast majority of people end up losing money, often thousands of dollars. This is because the MLM business model is inherently flawed. It relies on a constant influx of new recruits in order to sustain itself, which is not sustainable in the long run.

Another reason why Amway recruits people is because they know that there are many people out there who are in need of a job. With the job market becoming increasingly competitive, many people are struggling to find work. Amway offers these people an alternative to traditional employment. They promise them a flexible schedule, the ability to work from home, and the opportunity to be their own boss.

While this may sound appealing to some people, the reality is that working for Amway is not the same as having a traditional job. Amway independent business owners are not employees of the company. They are independent contractors who are responsible for their own expenses, including marketing materials, training, and travel. They are also responsible for building their own downline, which requires a significant amount of time and effort.

Furthermore, Amway independent business owners are not protected by the same labor laws as traditional employees. They are not entitled to minimum wage, overtime pay, or benefits like health insurance or paid time off. They are also not protected by anti-discrimination laws, which means that they can be discriminated against based on their race, gender, or other factors.

Amway recruits people for a variety of reasons, but the two main reasons are when people need money and when they are in need of a job. While Amway offers people the promise of financial independence and the ability to work from home, the reality is that very few people actually make money through the company. The MLM business model is inherently flawed and relies on a constant influx of new recruits in order to sustain itself. Amway independent business owners are not protected by the same labor laws as traditional employees and are often left to fend for themselves.

The Lies

You don't need to sell these products in stores in order to sell a lot.

If we don't need to sell a product in stores, then why do we even have stores in the first place? They only say this because it will make them more money to sell them online. It's not like they have not make enough money from signup costs already.

<u>Ditto ordering will help you, and our team</u>

Note: "Ditto ordering" is An Amway term for ordering the same product automatically each month on a certain day.

When my recruiter told me this, I was confused. How could ordering from my own storehelp us stand as a group? When I asked him, I got nowhere. I got answers that didn't make any sense, and that's when I realized that this was all bullshit. If you are told that making an order automatically every month is good for your business, then they're bullshiting you, because all you'll do is waste money, and invest in someone else other than yourself.

Our products are like no other

Every Multi-Level Marketing company says this same exact thing. *You will lose weight if you buy our protein shakes! That belly fat will be gone if you buy our wraps! Your hair will grow back if you buy our shampoo!* Do any of those sayings sound like a company you've heard of? Maybe it's Monat? Herbalife? itWorks? All of those companies are Multi-level-marketing companies that do the exact same thing. They tell you that the products they sell are like no other, and get you to spend money on them, when in reality, they suck.

The products will sell themselves

This is just one, big, fat lie. The products are complete garbage and have the same quality as something you pick up at the dollar store. If I learned anything from marketing class in High School, it's that the product must be in demand in order for it to sell themselves. If the products would sell themselves, then people would be knocking down your door, wanting you to take their money for that shampoo, or that protein shake, or that bottle of essential oils.

The American Way

You can take time off when you want to! You don't have to ask permission from your boss to go get a haircut!

So, after being in the corporate world for almost a year, I can safely say that the people who say this have NEVER had a corporate job. With MY corporate job, I can tell my boss "Hey, I'm going to lunch" or "Hey, I need to take care of something at the bank", and as long as there is nothing going on at that moment, my boss is 100% okay with it.

And that even goes to taking days off!

With my current position, I got hired at my 9-5 job though a contracting agency. So this means that I am an employee to the agency, but I'm considered a contractor to the 9-5 job. In the contract made by the agency and the job, they did not include vacation time in the contract. Which means that I am not eligible for it. But even if I need to take a day off, I can go to my boss on Monday, say I need off on Tuesday, and she would be like "Okay!"

Long story short, this argument is coming from a lot of people in MLMs who have *never* had a corporate job.

<u>Buy from your own store, to invest in your business</u>

I can still hear someone say "Why would you want to invest in someone else when you can buy from your store and invest in yourself! It's that easy!" and that can't be more of a lie. You are told that you are to buy from your own store, and you will see profit flow in. When I bought an $8 bottle of shampoo, you know how much I got out of it? $0.01! How is that investing in my business, when all you do is spend it all?! In the MLM industry, you are taught to manipulate the truth, and this is just one example.

You will make a butt-load of money, and be sitting on "the beaches of the world"

Unless you started out early in the game, youwill have a VERY low chance of having any success in Multi-Level Marketing. It is proven, that you have a better chance of hitting it big at the CASINO! And an even bigger chance in no-product, illegal pyramid schemes! Companies like Amway *want* you and your friends to spend money on them. Like I said before. At my "grand opening", One of my friends bought ninety-seven dollars worth of products. How much did I make off that sale? $13. The rest went to my upline and Amway. One of my coworkers bought some energy drinks for $33 (Including shipping), and I got a measly $1.14 from that sale. You guessed it. The rest went to my upline and Amway. They want you to buy products because it makes them money. *NOT YOU!*

If I sign you up, it's out of the goodness of my heart/I want to help you/I want to share this opportunity

Yeah right! When I was sitting at Panera with my friend, when he signed me up for Amway, he said he gets nothing for doing so. That may be true for the signup costs, but for whatever sale I make, he receives a cut off it. If I sell $1000 worth of products, I will receive little to nothing, and he will receive more than me, and it just goes up the pyramid. It's a complete lie that they make nothing from signing up.

Every company in existence runs like an MLM.

When people say this, they are referring to the **Corporate Hierarchy** and how it is pyramid shaped. This is NOT what we're talking about and have a problem with.

> Fun Fact: One time, I had a Primerica Sales Represenitive tell me this, and when I told her she was wrong and talking about the corporate hierarchy, she proceeded to tell me that my professor in college was wrong and that my job was a pyramid scheme as well.

Let me explain.

According to marketing91.com, the definition of the Corporate Hierarchy (Also referred to as the *Organizational Hierarchy*) is "…how an organization or a company is organized."

In almost EVERY company, the Corporate Hierarchy IS shaped in the shape of a pyramid…but it's something TOTALLY different than what we're referring to.

What WE'RE referring to is the **Business Structure.**

The Business structure refers to how the employee is paid. It doesn't matter id the employee is considered a contractor, or a full time/part time employee. The Business structure still applies.

In the case of Multi-Level Marketing companies, they have a "Pyramid Selling" business structure.

The means that the way the company makes money is from a contracted, non-salaried workforce. The earnings from each contracted sales employee are given to them from a "compensation plan".

Some of the red flags of the "Pyramid Selling" business structure are:

- Requiring someone to "refer" or "recruit" you into the company
- Encouraged to sign people up under them
- Getting paid MORE for recruiting than product sales
- Paying for their now products to promote

- Being paid on a commission-only pay structure, where the person who recruited you (and so on) gets a cut of your pay

That is NOT how a company that does not follow the "Pyramid Selling" business structure

> *Another way you might hear this argument is when they say or represent that "every job is a pyramid scheme" or "Your corporate job is a pyramid scheme.". They also might add on that "You have the CEO at the top, the VP below him, the executives below them, then the managers, then the employees"*
>
> *No matter how this argument is presented, it all translates to "Every company in existence runs like a multi-level-marking company."*

runs. A company hires you, and they will supply the uniforms, they will supply the training, and you aren't expected to buy their products to meet a goal. Was it mentioned that you get an hourly pay as well?

But if you are in disbelief that MLM sales reps say this, here is a below example from a group I manage on Facebook, where the MLM sales rep was arguing with a Moderator.

The American Way

\# 1 I would argue that a corporate structure is a pyramid scheme

\# 2 - a pyramid scheme is taking money from people without a product and convincing others to do the same. In MLM you have a product or multiple products that you sell.

have you ever in your life bought something and loved it so much you told your friends and family about it? Then you are a network (your friends/family) marketer (the product you told them about. The only difference is that you are making money for the companies that sold you those products and you received nothing in return.

100% not a scam, a job is a scam

<u>Buying cheap things to save money is a mindset that you need to get rid of.</u>

This is a lie I was told by the person that recruited me when I told him that my parents buy Wal-Mart Branded items. He responded that my parents were wrong and that they have a mindset of buying cheap things. He told me not to fall for that mindset.

This is simply wrong because it isn't a mindset. A mindset is usually a bad thing, but in this case, it's a smart thing. What would you rather do…Spend your money on products that work, and will save you money, or buy expensive products in bulk that are most of the time junk and don't do what they say? It's a no-brainer that you want to save money, and get products that work.

You're a real business owner

This one is just an insult to *real* business owners. People the own their own LLCs, or have a local bakery, or have a small publishing house put in a lot of money, time, and hard work into their business, and someone that works for these companies, comes around, and tried to sell them aproduct and call themselves "business owners". It's just wrong, and it's very insulting to the people who are *actual* business owners. Paying a company to become a commission-only salesperson is *not* the same as putting your blood, sweat, and tears into starting an ACTUAL business.

If you sign up under me, you're an entrepreneur

If I could post a meme in this book, I would. That meme would be the lady trying to solve the complicated math problems because that's how my brain feels looking back when I knew *nothing* about Multi-Level-marketing.

According to Investopedia.com, an Entrepreneur is "an individual who creates a **new business**, bearing most of the risks and enjoyingmost of the rewards. The entrepreneur is commonly seen as an **innovator**, a source of **new ideas**, goods, services, and business/orprocedures."

I bolded the text in that quote that proves you're not an entrepreneur if you sign up for Amway.

If you become an Amway IBO, you are not starting a NEW business, but you are paying to expand a multi-million dollar corporation. You're not being innovative, because you do not set the rules that Amway and your upline forces you to follow, and your new ideas are not going to be implemented (Unless, MAYBE, you're in the top 0.4% of the successful people in the business) because they see you as someone they can get rid of any time. I mean, you get paid pennies to the dollar, so if they get rid of you, there's no harm to them.

<u>The people that quit Amway didn't work hard enough in their business</u>

I do admit that if you don't work hard enough while starting an actual business you call your own, you won't go anywhere. That is true, but saying this while being an Amway IBO doesn't make sense.

Firstly, saying that implies that you're an *actual business owner*, which is *far* from true.

The next reason why it doesn't make any sense is because of how the company is structured.

Every time you make a sale, buy something, or spend any money in the business, your Upline gets a cut off the sale, and their upline gets a cut, and so on and so forth. No matter how hard you work, you will make literal pennies, compared to opening an *actual* business.

You can pass me, or my upline, if you work hard enough

This goes with the last point I mentioned. You *cannot* rank past your upline unless they quit. Andsince they have you under their belt and they're making money off you, I doubt they will. As I stated before, the money that you make off a sale just goes up the latter (Or Pyramid), and the people at the top get most of the money off what not only the customers purchases, but what YOU buy as well, and even when you recruit someone and they buy their "starter kit"

Side note: MLM sales reps will says this as a rebuttal to why they MLM is not a pyramid scheme.

This argument has NOTHING to do with what makes a company a pyramid scheme. Please see the "We're not a pyramid scheme" point for more information.

The starter kit is an investment to jumpstart your business

Far from the truth, Hun. The starter kit is just filled with the products that you would try and push your family and friends to buy, or worse, have them sell under you. I remember riding home with my upline, and they said that it was optional to get, but it would be a *great* investment for me, so I can build my "business".

If you don't support my Multi-level Marketing business, you're just a hater / jealous of me / a bully

If I had a dollar for every time I heard this, I would have enough money for rent for a month.

There's a difference between not only criticism about your company and being an *actual* bully, but also there's a difference between criticism against the company you work with, and criticism towards you or your decisions.

People in MLMs tend to mix the two, and are brainwashed to believe that anything bad that is said about the company they work with is considered "hateful" and they need to cut them out of their life.

I have also provided another comment from the Facebook group I moderate from a different MLM rep.

██████ good sir, it is not an MLM. I don't need to sign anyone up to sell anything and I don't get paid if anyone decides to hang their hat/license with the company. Because since this is legitimate you have to actually get licensed by your state to do it.

Again, I appreciate your questions. However, I am cutting negative people out of my life. So unless you have an actual question I am afraid I'm done with our exchange. Have a great evening!

We're not a pyramid scheme

That is debatable…

The reason I state this is because of a statement from the FTC. According to the FTC, in order for a company to be considered a pyramid scheme is when A majority of the one made by a participant is from recruiting and NOT product sales.

We have many MLM companies as an example. One of them being AdvoCare and Success By Health. These two companies were shut down by the FTC for being Illegal pyramid schemes, and they had the EXACT same business structure as any other MLM company. Including Amway.

And as mentioned before, MLMs have a "Pyramid Selling" business structure. The SAME structure as an illegal pyramid scheme.

Some MLM reps may say things that depot have to do with how a company is classified as a pyramid scheme, such as "I can pass my spline, so that doesn't make it a pyramid scheme", but most of the time what they say has NOTHING to do with the company being identified as a pyramid scheme.

As stated before, in order for a company to be considered a pyramid scheme is when A majority of the one made by a participant is from recruiting and NOT product sales.

Conclusion

If you want to have a legit job that you can make a decent amount of income with, AND still stay in the comfort of your own home, there are plenty of companies out there that will offer that.

But Amway is not one of those.

If you are planning to use Amway as a side hustle to make a few extra bucks, I have written *"Beyond the Veil: 65 side hustles to make money, rather than multi-level marketing"*, which tells you about side hustles you can do and not be sucked into one of these schemes.

To make a short story even shorter, **don't do Amway…Or any MLM…**

www.ingramcontent.com/pod-product-compliance
Lightning Source LLC
Chambersburg PA
CBHW030448220526
45464CB00006B/2447